A Kid's Guide to Helen Keller
An Book Just for Kids

eKids Press

www.eKidsPress.com

An Imprint of Minute Help, Inc.

© 2012. All Rights Reserved.

Table of Contents

About eKids

Adults! Turn away! This book is not for you!
eKids Books is proud to present a new series of
books for all the readers who matter the most:
Kids, of course!

Introduction

Who was Helen Keller and why is she so important? Well, imagine being able to read, speak, and write just like everyone else that you know, but also imagine that you learned to do these things even though you are blind and deaf! Helen Keller was able to not only learn to speak, read, and write but she also wrote more than ten books, spoke to large crowds of people, traveled all around the world, and even met 12 United States Presidents!

This was not done in the modern day with all of the electronic devices and well-developed systems that we have for people with a visual or hearing handicap. It all began back in the 1880s when Helen Keller was a very young girl! Helen Keller is important to us today because she proved that almost anything is possible if you really set your mind to it. Consider that she learned several different languages, graduated from Radcliffe College and worked with many organizations created to support people struggling with disabilities. She was more than brave and courageous...she was a hero.

Like all heroes, however, Helen Keller faced some major challenges, and they all began when she was less than two years old...

Chapter 1: What was Helen Keller Like as a Kid?

Helen Keller was born in June of 1880 and was considered to be a "normal" baby. That means that she was born with vision and hearing that worked just fine. When she was nineteen months old, however, she came down with something that doctors called "brain fever". Both her stomach and her brain had some sort of major infection, and doctors today believe she must have had a very severe case of scarlet fever or meningitis. Either condition could have easily killed her, but little Helen survived.

In the days after her recovery, her mother noticed that Helen was not acting like normal. She did not react when someone spoke to her, and she acted as if she did not see you if you waved a hand in front of her face. Was she acting? No...her illness had left her deaf and blind.

First Friends

Little Helen did not stop communicating at that time, however, and would use what are called "home signs" to speak with a six-year old friend named Martha Washington. The home signs that Helen used were all different and things that she made up on her own. That is something that often happens when a child cannot hear and is not trained in sign language.

So, little Helen would make up gestures and movements of her hands when she was trying to say something. She would always use the same movements to mean the same things, but it was not a way of speaking that she could ever use outside of her family home.

When she was only seven years old her family knew around sixty different home signs that Helen had created. This was not going to be enough to give Helen a full life, however, and her parents wanted to find a better solution.

Finding Answers for Helen

Helen's mother, Kate, was young and very active. She wanted to give Helen as many opportunities for a good life as possible and was inspired by something that she found in the book American Notes that author Charles Dickens had written after visiting the United States. In it, he talked about a doctor in Baltimore, Maryland who had worked wonders with little Laura Bridgman - a "deafblind" child. (Being "deafblind" means that someone has no vision and no hearing. The name was created because someone who is deafblind is going to have a life and life experiences that are very different from people who are only deaf or only blind.)

The doctor in Baltimore sent them on to inventor Alexander Graham Bell who was in the process of learning the best ways to educate deaf children. He had already invented the telephone, but had dedicated his work to helping children who had no hearing. The inventor told the Kellers that the person to contact for help was Michael Anagnos, who was the director of the Perkins Institution and Massachusetts Asylum for the Blind.

Why? Bell knew that Anagnos would probably be able to give them the best advice about Helen's options for education of any kind. So, they took Bell's advice and headed to see Mr. Anagnos. He consulted with them, met Helen, and immediately recommended one of his former pupils as a tutor or "live in" teacher for Helen.

Would it work? That was a big question because young Helen was already a bit of a challenge. For example, as she was growing and trying to learn, she would stand between people who were having a conversation and put her hands on their mouths. She couldn't understand them and would get incredibly angry and frustrated. In her own biography, she wrote about her tremendous temper tantrums in which she "kicked and screamed until...exhausted". In other words, she got out of hand and very wild on a regular (sometimes a daily) basis.

Imagine trying to be the teacher of a young child so full of rage, but also imagine being Helen. She didn't understand that "words" meant "things". She wanted to communicate, but she had no way of doing it, and she was very, very smart!

Chapter 2: The Arrival of Anne Sullivan

So, in March of 1887 Anne Sullivan moved into the Keller's home in Alabama and began to try to teach Helen how to use her hands to sign. Anne was using American Sign Language, which is a very well-designed system of hand and arm movements that are used instead of spoken words. It was designed for people who are only deaf or have no hearing.

How, you might wonder, did a child like Helen learn sign language or ASL if she could not see the hand signs and movements? The way that Helen was taught was by touch. Her teacher put her hand inside of Helen's palm and made the movements.

Imagine this for a moment...you cannot see or hear, but you know that people do make sounds and talk. You don't really know how to talk like that, and then suddenly someone keeps holding your hand and rolling their fingers around in the palm of it. What does that mean? What are they doing?

It is not surprising that Helen was often upset and angry with Anne because she didn't understand things. For example, there is a famous story of Anne putting a doll in Helen's hand and then using sign language to spell "D-O-L-L" in the other hand. For a long time Helen was very annoyed by Anne's spelling because she did not yet realize that each item or idea in the world had words that were used to explain them or to describe them. She did not know that a doll was called a doll, or that words were called words. She recognized the movements that Anne did for "doll" and for "cake," but she was not really understanding what they meant. One day, Anne was trying to teach Helen to use the word "M-U-G" for a mug of water, but Helen became enraged and ended up breaking her own precious doll during a tantrum. Of course, if you think about Helen's world, it is easy to understand her anger and frustration.

This did not make things easy on the people around her though, and Anne asked if she and Helen could live in a small cottage away from the family homestead until Helen's manners could be improved. For one thing, Anne was very upset by Helen's horrible table manners. Consider that anyone sitting down to dinner with Helen would have to watch her eat only with her hands and would have to accept it if she reached out and took all of the food from their plate. Anne felt that she was living with a wild animal sometimes, and so she tried very hard to "tame" her.

She taught Helen how to take care of herself. She learned to button her shoes and brush her hair, but her temper tantrums did not stop. So, Anne would refuse to use sign language when Helen's behavior got too naughty or wild. Though the two began to become friends, things got pretty bad before Helen had what Anne called a "breakthrough".

The Famous Breakthrough

One day, Anne was making the movements for "W-A-T-E-R" on Helen's palm as she poured water over the other hand. Suddenly, as Helen remembered in her autobiography, she realized that those movements meant "water" and that her teacher was putting letters together to make a "word," and that the word was describing the "water" pouring over her hand.

Helen wrote, "Suddenly I felt a misty consciousness as of something forgotten, a thrill of returning thought, and somehow the mystery of language was revealed to me". It was if a dam broke open and Helen almost exhausted her teacher in the days to come as she dragged her all over the family farm demanding that she give a name and the signs for the many different objects, items, and materials to be found there. One of the nicest things that happened on the day of Helen's breakthrough was that she asked for Anne's name, and Anne also gave her the word "teacher," too. In only a few hours, Helen had added 30 new words and signs to her vocabulary.

In the next few days, it became very clear that Helen had always been misbehaving simply because she was so remarkably clever and smart. She learned at a speed that her teacher did not believe was possible. In almost no time at all, Helen was learning to read in the two ways that the blind had available: by raised letters and by the Braille system.

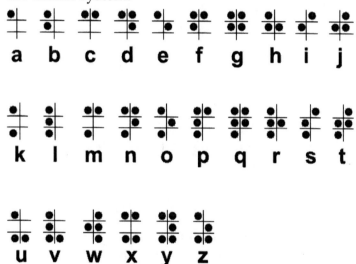

Braille Reading

Helen learned to read in Braille, which is a very common system used by people with visual impairment. It can be used for reading and writing if you have a special typewriter. It was created by Louis Braille in 1825 and uses small raised dots to stand for regular letters. For example, each of the Braille letters is made up of two columns of three dots each. The dots are raised in specific places to mean a letter. The letter "A" is two raised dots in the first column, etc.

So, just like regular school kids learn to read and write, Anne was teaching Helen how to do the same thing, but using sign language and Braille.

Helen's Progress

The progress that Helen had made so quickly was reported back to Mr. Anagnos (remember he had recommended Anne as Helen's teacher). He was amazed at the speed that Helen was learning and he wrote an article about it to discuss the methods being used. This brought a lot of attention, and Helen was actually photographed many times and appeared in all kinds of American newspapers.

This made her a bit of a celebrity, and it was decided that the best thing for her was an education at a regular school. So, in 1890, Helen and Anne had moved to the Perkins Institute in Watertown, Massachusetts. Anne was still her companion and teacher, but there were other teachers and students there for Helen to work with as well. This is the reason that, soon after they arrived, Helen was going to be taught how to speak as well as to read and write.

By the age of ten she had started to develop the ability to speak, but was not easy to understand if you were not used to her voice and the way she made sound. Over time, however, this would improve. Remember, she was only ten years old, and had only started to learn words and letters at the age of eight!

In 1894, Helen and Anne relocated to New York in order for Helen to be able to study at two different schools. She would enroll in the Wright-Humason School for the Deaf and the Horace Mann School for the Deaf. The two women had been introduced to Dr. Wright and Dr. Humason because they had just created their school in order to teach speech to children who did not hear. They had a bit of success with Helen, but it would be a few more years before she was speaking clearly.

By 1896, Helen was 16 years old and thinking about her formal education. She and Anne moved on to Cambridge School for Young Ladies. She was there for a few years and was accepted to Radcliffe College (which was the women's version of Harvard University) in 1900. This meant that Helen had not only learned to read, write, and speak, but had become a very strong scholar, too!

Unfortunately, as Helen's constant companion, Anne had to help her with studies. She was someone who was also visually impaired (which many people did not know) and all of the reading and writing that was done to help Helen took a very big toll on Anne's eyesight.

Helen graduating from Radcliffe

Chapter 3: A Career in Writing

Now, just stop to think for a few moments. Helen had not spoken or communicated until she was eight. She did not learn to speak until after the age of eleven, and yet by the time she was twenty years old she was entering into a very tough college.

This shows just what kind of person Helen Keller was. She may have been an extremely difficult child who had a lot of temper tantrums and who behaved like a wild animal, but it was all because of her frustration at being unable to communicate.

Once Helen could learn, she just gobbled up information wherever she could find it. She had a very active mind, and even while she struggled with college classes, she was thinking about writing her life's story.

Friends and Companions

It is very interesting to learn that one of Helen's biggest fans during her time in college was the famous American writer Mark Twain. He was amazed at Helen's courage and intelligence, and tried to support her amazing efforts. He introduced her to his friends, and this is the reason that she was able to go to such a famous school as Radcliffe College.

Remember that Helen's family were farmers from Alabama who had a comfortable life but no real riches to spend on things like a college education. So, Twain introduced Helen to an oil company owner named Henry Huttleston Rogers and his wife Abby. They were so impressed with Helen that they paid for her entire college tuition!

This made it possible for her to become the very first deafblind person to receive a Bachelor's Degree, but Helen had even bigger plans. She had graduated in 1904, but before that she was trying to write her life's story (in Braille and with a regular typewriter!) and she and Anne decided to approach a publisher for some help.

This is when they met John Albert Macy, who edited and published Helen's very first book in the year before she completed college. "The Story of My Life" was not an instant success, but it has gone on to be one of the most popular books that Helen completed.

Soon after Helen graduated from school, Anne and John Macy decided to get married. This did not mean that Helen lost her childhood teacher and friend, however, and the three of them lived in a home in Wrentham, Massachusetts.

This was a good arrangement for Helen because it allowed her to continue writing, and in the years that she shared a home with the couple, she would write the other book that she is famous for, "The World I Live In". This was the first book in which Helen felt free to write about the many things she felt about the world, including things like politics, social problems, and more.

After only a few years of marriage, Anne and John's relationship did not work out. He moved out of their home in 1914, and at the same time, they decided to hire someone to help around the house. This was Polly Thompson, who would also become a constant companion to Helen in later years.

By 1914, Helen was no longer a kid and had published her third book, "Out of the Dark," which also had a lot of her personal opinions and thoughts. This led to a new direction in her and Anne's lives, and the two would soon start touring the world to give lectures.

Chapter 4: Who was Anne Sullivan?

What is interesting to many people is the story of Anne Sullivan. After all, who was she? Why did she commit her entire life to Helen Keller? Anne's story is not the happiest tale, and begins with tragedy.

She was born to very poor parents in 1866. Thomas and Alice Sullivan could not read or write and had almost no money. When Anne was only eight years old her mother died and little Anne was sent to an "almshouse," or a charity house to live with her younger brother and sister. Sadly, her brother died only a short time after their father left them at the almshouse. Young Anne was blind due to an untreated medical condition known as trachoma, but she showed such intelligence and ability to learn that she was sent for a meeting at the Perkins School for the Blind and met her teacher Michael Anagnos. At that meeting she was so desperate to go to school that she threw herself on the ground in front of the Chairman, Mr. Frank Sanborn, and cried out: "Please, Mr. Sanborn, I want to go to school!"

She was accepted and placed with Mr. Anagnos as her teacher. This is the same teacher who would recommend Anne to be Helen's teacher only a few years later at the age of 20.

Was Anne totally blind? No; she regained most of her eyesight after going through several operations. She graduated at the very top of her class in 1886, and was soon teaching Helen Keller.

Life With Helen

We know that she became Helen's companion for almost 50 years, even after she herself had married and moved into a home of her own. The question that a lot of people ask is why Anne remained such a dedicated friend.

The answer is actually very easy: Anne was just as amazed by Helen's intelligence and courage as everyone who knew her. The thing that made their relationship so unique and different is that it was Anne who finally broke through the wall that Helen had been trapped behind due to her deafblindness. This created a bond that would never break, and an understanding between the two women that was similar to the relationship between brothers and sisters or children and parents.

Anne had come from a terrible background. She was not raised with any real family and had been trapped in blindness for many years of her life, too. She was committed to Helen as a teacher, friend, and companion because the two really were just like family to each other.

It is sad to know that some people thought that Anne was trying to control Helen, but that is nonsense. There was simply no one who could ever control Helen Keller. Anne simply remained by her side to ensure that Helen could accomplish all of the great things that she did during her lifetime.

She even remained with Helen when she took to the stage later in life as a vaudeville performer! It is easy to see that she was not trying to control her friend, but to instead provide her with protection and companionship.

Teaching Helen

We should also remember that the first things that Anne taught Helen were things that very few people even understood. For example, remember that the pair had to use the "manual alphabet". This was the sign language that Anne used on Helen's palm and which was totally different from the traditional American Sign Language that Anne had been using for her many years of school.

Remember too that Anne was not only working as a teacher in a classroom. She was working with an almost wild child in a situation that very few teachers would accept. All of that proves that Anne was dedicated first to teaching and then to Helen. She was a teacher in her heart, and this is the only thing that allowed her to break through to Helen.

It is not surprising that this would create a very strong bond between the two women, and that it would last them for the rest of their lives.

Anne as a Miracle Worker

Just consider the words that Helen wrote about Anne:

"By nature she was a conceiver, a trail-blazer, a pilgrim of life's wholeness. So day by day, month after month, year in and year out, she labored to provide me with a diction and a voice sufficient for my service to the blind."

Helen Keller admits that it was only through Anne's services that she could become the person that she was. We already understand that Anne worked very hard to overcome her sad history and physical limits, but we should also understand that she was doing all of this in a time when women and poor people were usually not allowed to do much in life.

For example, in the middle to late 1800s a single woman from a poor background would usually end up working in a factory setting and not going to school at all. Anne's blindness and the way her father abandoned her and her brother and sister actually put her in a position to break away from the normal pattern. She did go to school, and she lived a life that was entirely different from other women in her same situation.

Anne as Wife and Companion

We have to also consider what Anne did after she finished teaching Helen. She followed her to college and helped her with her studies. She helped her to begin her writing career. When she married John Macy, she demanded that he too learn the manual sign language necessary to communicate with Helen - this was because he was helping her write an autobiography and Anne wanted it to be entirely in Helen's own words.

Helen said that the first few years of Anne's marriage were among the happiest in their lives together. They were working and living life just like a normal family, and Anne had even made sure that all of the legal and financial issues in Helen's life would be managed properly if Anne happened to die before her new husband.

A very important thing happened at this time as well, and it is something that proves how little "control" Anne ever tried to have over Helen. The two women each took an interest in politics as they got older, and they both had very different ideas. Anne was known to never interfere with Helen in any way where her political activities were concerned!

The first signs of trouble began in 1913 when Anne and Helen accepted a lecturing tour that would last for 15 months. This was necessary due to financial problems, and the tour would help to solve them.

This long time apart upset the marriage between John and Anne, and by 1914 he had moved to a new home of his own. He never returned to life with the two women, but John and Anne never divorced, either.

Anne as Educator

As the years passed there were many who began to understand the great work Anne had done with Helen, and to see that Anne was a very amazing teacher and educator. There were several magazine articles, and in 1915, Anne was given a special Teacher's Medal at an International Exposition. Unfortunately, the fun and excitement of this time was overshadowed by John's departure and by the fact that Anne's vision began to fail.

She had developed pleurisy and now it was Anne who needed some care. She travelled to a special clinic in Puerto Rico and spent five months recovering from her condition. The vacation helped her greatly, and she returned home in good spirits.

By 1917, she was fit enough to do another lecturing tour with Helen, and this one was all about the war that was raging in Europe. Now, both Anne and Helen would visit with World War I soldiers who had been blinded during a battle and would continue to speak out about the great evils of war.

It is hard to imagine, but life got even busier for Anne and Helen in the years 1917 and onward. They traveled, they went to Hollywood and they met all of the American Presidents starting with Coolidge. They even began to deliver funny performances known as "vaudeville" to continue to make some money and stay active with the public.

By the 1920s, they were involved in a major speaking campaign for the American Foundation for the Blind, but by 1930, Anne's vision was very bad. She trained their housekeeper and companion Polly Thompson to use the manual sign language, and in 1928 Anne struggled to help Helen complete another book. In 1932, Anne was given an honorary degree from Temple University in Pennsylvania, but her health had gotten very bad. Sadly, she lost her sight about one month before she died in 1936. She and Helen are buried together.

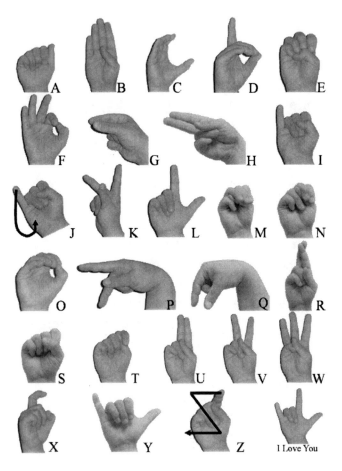

Chapter 5: How Does Sign Language Work?

Now that you understand a bit about Helen Keller and her teacher Anne Sullivan you probably want to know just how sign language works. Firstly it starts with an alphabet, and most people who use sign language in the United States will rely on the American Sign Language alphabet.

This is done entirely through the use of hand gestures, and all of the letters and numbers use only a single hand. This makes many people wonder how you can just stand there "writing" or spelling words with your hand, but that is not actually how sign language works.

Why not? Well, there are also all of the "words," too. For instance, there are signs that mean different words, and these are put together to make sentences. What is so interesting about American Sign Language, or ASL, is that it also asks the speaker to show all kinds of facial expressions to explain the "emotion" of the sentence, too.

For example, if you were telling an action story in sign language you would never just stand there with no expression on your face and make the signs. You would, instead, wave your hands about, make faces that showed excitement and drama, and really act out the story a bit, too.

This is why you could stand and watch someone use sign language to tell a story and understand easily if it was a funny, scary, sad, boring, or action filled story. This is also why sign language is a very common way for those without hearing to communicate.

Different Languages

Okay, you might think, "what about people who speak a different language than me?" Well, there are a few types of sign language in addition to American Sign Language. For example, there is actually British Sign Language and French Sign Language. What is interesting to know is that the French and American versions are very close, and that means that most "speakers" of these different languages can communicate with one another.

You should also know that the "natural" or "home signs" that many deaf children create are never similar to formal sign languages. This is because one child may stomp when they want milk while another discovers that waving their hand up and down gets them a glass of milk. This is why you cannot compare home signs to regular sign languages.

A Bit of History

Though there have been deaf people since the beginning of human beings, there has not always been a sign language for them to use. Today's ASL is actually the result of the French Sign Language, or FSL. This was created only in the 1800s by a hearing man who worked with the deaf. He brought his discovery to the United States where the American School for the Deaf began to use it. Soon, this became the ASL that is still used today!

Because of the creation of the sign languages, there are also many special schools for people who are deaf. These schools have brought about many different systems for people who cannot hear or who are simply "hard of hearing" (meaning that they have a bit of hearing) and this has greatly improved the lives of millions of people.

Speaking in Signs

So, we know that there is a sign alphabet and many sign words and phrases. We also have to understand that there are other gestures, movements, and expressions that are used with sign language. Don't forget that another part of ASL is to move the mouth and silently speak the words being said. This is to help those who are "lip readers," too.

There are a lot of signs, however, that do not take a lot of training to understand. For example, if you wanted to tell someone that you were hungry in sign language you could use the word for "eat" - which is to put your fingers together as if you were pinching something with your fingertips, and to then move those fingers towards your mouth. This says "eat"! There are many examples of signs that are simply a bit of acting or miming of the word. The same can be said about the alphabet, with many of the signs looking almost exactly like the written letters. What is interesting to know is that few people learn sign language in a way that connects to reading.

What does that mean? Well, someone who is deaf and learning to sign might not immediately say "Oh, the sign for 'W' looks just like a 'W'!" because they are not thinking of written letters at all.

Making it Work

If you are using sign language, you are probably doing a few different things as you speak. These things might include:

- Doubling - If you mean to say that someone is doing something you may have to repeat the sign twice. For example, if you say someone is "running" you would actually sign "run, run".

- Adding inflections - You can say the words "he is annoyed" or you can say "wow, he is very annoyed!" Someone using ASL can sign "he is annoyed" but use their facial expressions to mean "Wow, he is very annoyed!". You can also use a different speed to bring meaning to a sign. For instance, you can use the sign for run very slowly to mean that someone is a slow runner.

- Direction - If you want to say something in sign language that was about someone to that person, such as "I gave you this banana," you would only have to use the word for give and banana, and just move your hands towards that person to communicate the meaning.

- Finger Spelling - There is not always a sign for a word, and you might have to spell the word using very fast finger movements

Of course, it is not as simple as that. There is also very complicated grammar and even proper manners to use when communicating with ASL or any other sign language.

Now, imagine being blind and deaf and being able to learn all of the words, letters, numbers, grammar, and ways of making sign language work...that is precisely what Helen Keller was able to do all before the age of 15!

Chapter 6: What Was Helen Keller Like as an Adult?

You may think that all of the things Helen Keller did before the age of 25 were quite enough, but that is far from the end of the story.

Yes, by the time she was in her 20s she had learned to read, write and speak, but she had also written a few books and was about to begin speaking in public!

As an adult, Helen lived with Anne and her husband John. They worked together to write her books of essays and her autobiographies. By 1913, she had several books in print, but she was about to become known just as much for her speaking, her support for all people with disabilities, and her belief in the social model known as "socialism". She was also going to become known as a "suffragist" which was a woman who fought for the right to cast votes in elections.

Clearly, Helen had a lot to say and decided to say it herself rather than in a new book. So, in 1915 she began the Helen Keller International organization that would work to support research in health, vision and nutrition. She also made herself available for a 15-month lecture tour in 1913 as well. This began many years of globetrotting as Helen and Anne began speaking out about many issues, not only Helen's remarkable life story, but everything from poverty to unfair treatment of the disabled.

Taking to the Stage

In only a few short years of lecturing, however, there was little demand for Helen's speaking engagements. This had mostly to do with the fact that the United States had just completed its participation in World War I and many did not want to hear about the problems of the world. To continue to keep their concerns in the spotlight, however, Anne and Helen accepted work in a comedy show known as vaudeville. This was a bit of a scandal at the time because the shows were not seen as entirely proper for all ages. This did not concern Helen at all and she was more than happy to relive her life's story over and over for the large audiences to enjoy.

This led to people from Hollywood contacting Helen and asking her and Anne to write a movie about her life. This was called "Deliverance," and it was not a huge success. That was fine for Helen, however, and she kept right on doing the vaudeville shows, and also adding a "question and answer" section that let the audience ask her about the different things she thought and experienced in her life.

Back to Normal

By 1919, the two had earned enough to return home and to even purchase a bigger house in Forest Hills, New York. Now it was only Anne and Helen because John Macy (Anne's husband) had moved into a home of his own. They had decided to hire help, and Polly Thompson soon became a permanent part of their lives.

This was good news because Helen began to work with one of her favorite organizations of them all, the American Foundation for the Blind. She helped them to earn money and she went on different speaking tours to make sure that people understood the many challenges that blind people faced.

Sadly, all of the way back in 1914, Anne's health began to crumble. By 1922, it was time for Polly to step in as a sort of secretary and companion to Helen, too. Together the "three musketeers," as they were often called, still traveled the world and met all kinds of celebrities.

Helen with President
Coolidge

Big Changes

In 1936, Anne Sullivan died. This was a huge
blow to Helen, but it did not stop her from
trying to improve the world around her. She and
Polly worked with the American Foundation for
the Overseas Blind during the years of World
War II, and together they visited Africa, South
America, Australia, Japan and more.

Now it was Polly's turn to become a bit
weakened by age and illness, and so the two
returned to their home in New York. The two
did not do as much traveling or activity from
that point onward, but Helen was still writing
and publishing some of her 13 books.

Polly died in 1960, and she was buried with
Anne Sullivan. It was her nurse who became
Helen's final companion. She remained with her
all of the rest of her life. It was not until a year
after Polly's death that Helen formally retired
from public service. In 1961, she suffered a
stroke and needed to remain at home in the care
of Winnie Corbally (Polly's nurse).

She received the Presidential Medal of Freedom in 1964 and was put in the Women's Hall of Fame at the New York World's Fair of 1965. She died at home in her sleep in June of 1968. Just like Polly, Helen was also buried alongside her nearly constant life companion, Anne Sullivan, in the National Cathedral in Washington, D.C. This spot is so popular with visitors and travelers that the Braille plaque marking her grave has had to be replaced twice since she died. Why? Millions of people have touched the raised Braille letters that spell her name, and have worn them down to nothing.

Clearly, this shows how beloved Helen Keller is to the modern world. She had lived for more than 85 years and had experienced two World Wars. She had created a foundation to help the blind, spoke to tens of thousands of people, and witnessed award winning plays and movies made about her. She demonstrated to the world that a disability, even a major disability, did not mean that you could not accomplish great things.

She lived in service to her fellow human beings, and is recognized today for her brilliant mind and her amazing spirit.

Conclusion

Did Helen Keller leave a legacy? Of course! Although the use of sign language and manual sign language would have most certainly continued had Helen Keller never lived, it was her use of them to break out of her silent and dark world that showed people just how far they could go.

Consider that Helen Keller and Anne Sullivan lived like two great scientists. They used what little technology they had to discover how to communicate with one another and the world. Through their work together and through Helen's writings, they were able to talk about the ways that the deaf, blind and deafblind experience the world. The honesty with which this was done demonstrated that any of these disabilities were not the end of the world. They also showed that someone with these disabilities had a lot to offer.

Consider this quote from Helen Keller as she explains the reason for her life's work:

"The public must learn that the blind man is neither genius nor a freak nor an idiot. He has a mind that can be educated, a hand which can be trained, ambitions which it is right for him to strive to realize, and it is the duty of the public to help him make the best of himself so that he can win light through work."

Web Resources

1. A Braille dictionary: you can see the full Braille alphabet when you visit the following site: http://en.wikipedia.org/wiki/Braille

2. A biography of Anne Sullivan: a very detailed online biography of Anne Sullivan is available at this link: http://www.afb.org/asm/

3. A biography of Helen Keller: at this site you will find a "kid friendly" biography of Helen Keller: http://www.kidskonnect.com/subject-index/21-people/152-keller-helen.html

4. The Birthplace of Helen Keller: go online and visit Helen's childhood home by following this link: http://www.helenkellerbirthplace.org/helenkellerbio/helen_keller_birthplace2_bio.htm

5. The full text of "The Story of My Life": Read this classic book by Helen Keller

when you visit the following link:
http://www.gutenberg.org/ebooks/2397

6. The Helen Keller Foundation: this site gives you all of the details about the foundation, its projects, and all kinds of resources about Helen and Anne. Visit: http://www.helenkellerfoundation.org/about_HK.asp

7. Learn ASL: why not begin to learn the first 100 signs needed to speak ASL by visiting: http://www.lifeprint.com/asl101/pages-layout/concepts.htm

8. Learn how sign language works: all of the basics of ASL are explained in this multi-page tutorial at: http://people.howstuffworks.com/sign-language.htm

9. Quotes from Helen Keller: she said many amazing things and you can find a lot of quotes from her at: http://www.quotationspage.com/search.php3?Author=Helen+Keller&file=all2

10. Helen Keller resources: find all kinds of details about Helen and her life by visiting this site at: http://www.rnib.org.uk/aboutus/about sightloss/famous/Pages/helenkeller.asp x

CPSIA information can be obtained
at www.ICGtesting.com
Printed in the USA
LVOW10s1152300117
522576LV00016B/734/P